Investing

Your Manual For Basic Passive Investing And Financial Preparation For Life Events

(The Best Techniques For Becoming A Savvy Investor And Making Money)

Johnnie Morrison

TABLE OF CONTENT

Technical Analysis 1

Charting Guidelines And Trends 11

Establishing Your Real Estate Goals 37

Cheap Investments To Expand Your Portfolio 58

How Etfs Make Money 79

Tips And Techniques For Etf Investing 83

The Investment Armory 87

What Good Is Investing In Bitcoin? 104

Investing In Options: A Guide 118

How To Invest For Cash Flow 126

Technical Analysis

There are a few fundamentals that you need to be aware of regardless of the kind of vehicle you decide to use for your operations. The majority of the connections between this basic information and market behavior exist. You will be able to predict the movement of the prices more correctly and, as a result, make wiser trading judgments if you can learn to understand their behavior. It may be interesting to observe that some principles can always be applied to prices and their behavior on the market, independent of the value that is transacted there.

This may be explained by the fact that independent traders and investors are in charge of transient price changes. We may assert that prices are influenced by the activities of persons who invest in or trade values on the market and that these prices respond similarly to comparable inputs or stimuli. Technical analysis is a field of study that focuses on studying how prices behave, and being able to comprehend its fundamentals is one of the most important educational skills you'll need to be able to make wise financial judgments in the market.

Introduction to Technical Analysis

Technical analysis is a vast subject. For as long as you plan to work as a trader, if you choose to join the market and become an investor, there is a good chance that you will find yourself returning to study and pick up new information often. Because of this, any expert in the field of options trading will tell you that learning the fundamentals of technical analysis is a crucial first step for anyone trading the market. You don't have to understand everything about it right soon, however. It is OK if, for certain areas of your company, you just investigate portions of the technical analysis that you are really interested in for that specific project since there is a vast field of research to be done. For instance, more than a hundred indicators are available for market analysis in technical analysis. In practice, traders often employ three or four, typically the most well-liked or simply the ones they were already acquainted with.

If you engage in trading generally rather than just option trading, you'll see that technical analysis may be used on any financial asset, such as stocks or futures, for instance.

They have their roots in psychology, human nature in general, and actual behavior, we may say. We will briefly review some of the major technical analysis issues in order to provide a better understanding. These subjects include:

The fundamentals of technical analysis, methods for charting trends and patterns, patterns used in technical analysis, technical analysis using averages movement, and indicators used in technical analysis.

Basis for Technical Analysis

The phrase "market action" serves as the primary foundation for technical analysis. Market activity is an indication of your overall understanding of the trading market; it excludes any information you would get from an insider. It may be summed up by saying that it is a research that identifies "the direction of the price movement over time." It also, if feasible, looks at its volumes and how they evolve over time.

However, the underlying tenet of technical analysis is that market behavior is a reflection of everything that has occurred and will happen with the price at a given point in time. The price is affected by a variety of factors, the magnitude of which varies on the market where the deal is done. Technical analysis steps in at this point and asserts that all of the information that may be known about the price is essentially already contained in the price that we see at the time that we wish to trade, cutting across all of those possibilities.

This implies you shouldn't worry too much about the factors that affect the price since, in accordance with this, all you need to do is watch how the price varies over time to find out the answers you need. Many individuals first questioned the viability of this sort of idea since it seemed so simple. Technical analysis is successful, despite the fact that this sort of definition doesn't appear that difficult, in case you had any worries.

One thing is clear from all of this, however, and it's crucial. Technical analysis cannot predict how the price will act. It may inform you that the price will rise or fall for a certain length of time, but this is not a guarantee. It may or might not. This is due to the fact that it is difficult to predict the market's behavior with absolute certainty, regardless of the calculations that must be made. The market operates in its own manner and ultimately fulfills its objectives. The only certainty you have from technical analysis is whether the law of probability is on your side or not since it provides you with an indicator of what will be the most likely conclusion.

You may engage in a lot of ordinary deals and perhaps turn a profit, but you should never risk money or important assets like your home or vehicle if you can't afford to lose them. It is not advised, particularly if one profitable transaction has convinced you that only one may serve as a reliable technical signal for a definite profit. This is one of the reasons why the first step in technical analysis is to analyze pricing and market behavior in order to increase your chances of success.

The second justification for the study is the fact that specific patterns are virtually always used to predict price changes. For instance, if the price rises, its tendency will be to continue rising unless something prevents it from doing so. Prices behave similarly to Newton's law of motion, which states that a body in motion will remain in motion until acted upon by an external force. Naturally, it must develop through time in order to demonstrate this. The price charts shown in many assessments wouldn't look the way they do if this weren't the case. They would be represented by the prices fluctuating at random. Technical analysis assumes that history will repeat itself, which is the third reason. It is quite likely that the same event will occur in the future if certain circumstances that occurred in the past are repeating themselves in the present. The second obvious consequence would be that because individuals are not anticipated to change in this equation, their outcomes would also be the same. This was, in a nutshell, the basic basis of technical analysis. Remember that using the majority of the information provided by this research is one of the most effective strategies to improve your trading skills and raise your chances of being a successful trader.

Several objections are made against the use of technical analysis. The fact that this analysis works and, at the very least, increases your chances of making greater percentages when trading is the only evidence you really need. We shall however highlight a few of the views regarding technical analysis:

"Charts only indicate what has occurred in the past, how can they reflect what hasn't happened yet," said one of the traders. The explanation is straightforward: there is data from prior transactions that is employed in technical analysis under the assumption that the past will repeat itself. In this manner, you can predict, at least with a degree of accuracy, what will happen to the price on the market in the future. In contrast, it functions similarly to the weather prediction; if it is predicted to rain on TV, even while you are aware that it may not, you nevertheless bring your umbrella with you. The same idea holds true for technical analysis, which is how previous occurrences may be used to forecast the future.

"If the prices already contain all there is to know, then any change in price can only come from fresh information that we don't know yet," said another dealer. This type of concept may be seen across the financial markets, not only in option trading. It comes up often, and scholars are still debating it. Contrary to the common belief among traders, this idea does not truly claim that the price that is presently being offered on the market is the right one. It simply claims that it is impossible to determine if the present price is too high or too cheap. Therefore, the best strategy for dealing with this idea is to provide evidence for how technical analysis really works. In the end, if everyone agreed with this sort of thinking, there would be no analysis and the cost would remain constant. Technical analysis seems to have self-fulfilling properties.

This implies that if the majority of traders do their analyses and determine that the price must rise, then all of them would start purchasing goods on the market, increasing demand and driving up the price. The price that is meant to decrease also operates along the same concept. This is another instance when technical analysis demonstrated its efficacy. Undoubtedly, there may be some skepticism, but is it really important to demonstrate why the price moved in the manner you anticipated it would? Additionally, if a big number of untrained traders who are just interested in making a fast profit fail, it may be assumed that the concept of having a large number of traders—regardless of their level of expertise and commitment—is flawed from the start.

Charting Guidelines And Trends

It is time to look at how the prices are charted or graphed and what those graphs represent once we have learned what the fundamentals of technical analysis are. This cannot be avoided, even if some may think it is not required. Throughout the course of your trading career, you will be required to see this kind of chart. If you go methodically, step by step, and attempt to keep in mind how these principles operate, it will be simpler to comprehend these concepts. There are a few different sorts of charts, but they all typically have a horizontal bottom and a vertical scale that is determined by time.

These charts are the only ones you should be interested in if you are just starting out since the price is often up to the side. You will look at the vertical line or period that most suits your trading strategy since it may be stated in minutes, days, or even weeks. However, as long as the other time scales are close to the values you selected, it is not uncommon for you to be interested in what occurs with them. In order to gain a more comprehensive view of what's going on the market, experienced traders often look at the other time frames. In this section, we'll discuss three different types of charts and assume that they all have the same time vertical axis and are expressed in the same currency.

Chapter 6: Be Willing to Take Chances (However, refrain from using money you'll soon need.)

You will at some time in the future experience investing losses. If you don't, you have merely been contributing to the Ponzi schemes' overall financial collapse. Investors always lose money; it's just part of the game. The investors who continue to profit in any market are either the luckiest individuals on the planet or, as has always been the case thus far, are engaged in some kind of illicit activity. Investors worried that Bernie Madoff could be participating in unlawful activity years before the Ponzi scheme was uncovered. This was established by examining his rates of return. It took years and the insolvency of Lehman Brothers for this to bring Madoff down. The figures on the books were too fantastic to be true, and so they were. Years ago, the knowledge might have been put to use, but regulatory panels chose to ignore it. You will sometimes lose money in your investments, and if you really never do, it may be time to take a deeper look at your holdings.

By clearly defining the amount of wealth you are ready to put in your investing strategy, you can best prepare for the risks you will need to take. Compared to your 401(k) or 529 savings plan, this will be different. You should indicate which assets are risk-free and which ones are in your layout. Separating this money can relieve a lot of your anxiety since you'll know you're protected from any bad investments. Your experimental money is the cash you have available for the stock market. This money might provide fantastic results, but you're ready to take some risks in order to learn which methods are most effective for you. Experiments (Risks) To Try

The stock market's individual equities are a fantastic area to test your cash. The stocks you choose should be determined by your study of the company's management and the underlying product it sells. Here, you may choose to take as much risk or as little. For instance, Apple was a sure bet a few years ago since they had a long list of items planned that were expected to generate significant profits. If you enter at the proper moment, riskier investments in lesser-known firms might potentially provide a sizable reward. As they try to entice new investors, smaller firms' payouts might also be proportionally rather substantial.

Another wonderful risk to take early on is short selling. The issue of a company generating annual dividends is less important here; the goal is to simply choose the companies you think will decline. This might indicate that you are seeing a broad market trend with a specific firm standing out as the first to fail in their industry. It could also signify that you think a business is overpriced. The idea of shorting Apple seemed ludicrous a few years ago, but it makes sense to take this risk now. Their stock has been gradually increasing for years, but the company's innovation has stalled.

I find it challenging to advise clients to buy penny stocks, but it is an alternative. Since each penny stock share is always worth less than $5 and often trades at or below a dollar, the risk associated with them is really fairly modest. This means that you may invest a lot in a little business and perhaps get incredibly tremendous payments if the business ever succeeds, but it is risky to gamble on a penny stock in the hopes of making a profit. The majority of penny stocks just provide poor chances, but if you have a good reason to think a business will expand rapidly, you may buy at the beginning with little money. Do keep in mind that it might be difficult to liquidate funds in penny stocks. Depending on the firm you buy shares in, but generally speaking, penny stocks are quite hard to unload.

Last but not least, an initial public offering, or IPO, might be a good place to start if you want to play with high yielding funds. Although IPOs provide the chance to make a lot of money, the majority of them fail. The firms that are still in business are the ones that people tend to remember from public offerings, but many more have only been prominent for a short while before disappearing entirely. Only if you really believe in a business and that its shares are inexpensive or are poised to grow in the future should you invest in it when it goes public. As huge corporations that the public has been familiar with for years are suddenly becoming publicly listed, many more investors are likely to get in on the first floor, which may be a trap for herds of investors. Facebook is the most recent illustration of this. Due to the enormous number of investors at the IPO, a firm like Facebook would soon become overpriced, and suddenly individuals who would never have been active in the stock market sought shares. Although the price of the Facebook shares first fell and took months to rise again, it now trades comfortably above its IPO. It is recommended to talk with a representative at your investment brokerage business if you are interested in an IPO since some IPOs are made accessible to the public while others are private.

Where to Purchase NFTs: 17 Market Places and What They Sell

Here's where to get your NFT fix, from memories to art to sports souvenirs.

Tesla CEO Elon Musk has standing bids of $10,000 or more for a number of his Twitter posts, including the timeless remark, "Was super fun tbh haha," on Valuables, an online market place for signed tweets recorded and verified on the Ethereum blockchain.

If that surprises you or if the burgeoning NFT market has you confused after hearing that a digital collage created by crypto artist Beeple sold for $69 million at Christie's, you're not alone.

NFT is an acronym for non-fungible taken. It is a digital asset that serves as a safe record of ownership for a thing or collection of things that is stored on certain blockchain ledgers like Ethereum and Solaris. NFTs are particularly useful for tracking ownership of immutable property, such as the rights to a picture or a piece of land, since they cannot be copied or altered.

Where To Buy Nfts | Axe Intelligence | Decembraland | Foundation | Grow.house

The Sandbox, Maker's Place, Mintable, NBA Top Shot, Nifty Gateway, Rarable, Sorare, SuperiorRare, Valuables, Venly, Zeptagram, and Zora are just a few of the apps and games available.

A dollar may be exchanged for any other dollar, and cryptocurrencies like bitcoin are no different. But an NFT functions differently. Like a rare postage stamp, a diary, or a 1952 Topps #311 Mickey Mantle, its value is based on its rarity and proof of origin.

Nearly anything may be listed as an NFT, including CryptoPunks blockheads, short films, domain names, and virtual cannab farms, but much of the recent enthusiasm among investors has been on digital art, collectible sports, and video games where players create and run parallel worlds, or "metaverses."

Where to Buy NFT

Today, the majority of NFTs are purchased using ETH, the cryptocurrency of the Ethereum network, which is easily converted to U.S. dollars on exchanges like Coinbase, Kraken, and Gemini.

Unlike bitcoin, which only functions as a payment network and cryptocurrency, blockchain networks like Ethereum and Solara allow users to create applications that can store personal data and establish rules for complex financial transactions, such as the smart contracts that control NFT ownership and sales.

To purchase NFTs, you must create a digital wallet where you may store your cryptocurrency. Examples include MetaMast, Binance, and Coinbase, which you may connect to the market place where you want to purchase NFTs (see below for market places to consider).

NFTs are often sold using an auction system in which you place a bid for the NFT. Some websites, such as OpenSea, provide the option to purchase the NFT right away for a set price.

Where to Purchase NFT

NFTs provide artists with a new market where they may sell their work and develop an automated method of recouping a percentage of sales via royalty agreements. Investors who are enthusiastic about the technology—a group that often overlaps with cryptocurrency enthusiasts—see NFTs as a means to invest in a market that is seeing staggering growth while also financially supporting artists.

Just how quickly is the market expanding? Market Watch said that in August 2021, the online market place OpenSea recorded $3.4 billion in transaction volume on Ethereum. And there is reason to assume that the NFT economy may be more than a passing trend given the amount of venture capital that is pouring into it from investors like Mark Cuban, Saleforce CEO Marc Benooff, and A16z Crypto.

Still, there have been several reports of theft and mania. Fees and costs vary widely, and the electricity required to power the Ethereum network comes from enormous carbon emissions. Those entering the market should do so with an open mind, understanding how crucial it is to assess market environments, including perhaps opaque FAQs and service terms.

With that in mind, if you're unsure of where to begin, take a look at these 17 marketplaces and what they have to offer both buyers and sellers.

SuperRare

A peer-to-peer marketplace called SuperRare allows users to buy and trade English-edited digital art. An Instagram profile-like tiling of windows that displays art, list prices, sale prices, and scheduled auctions. With top sellers like a Time Magazine cover selling for $300,000, the website is well-trafficked and home to a curated selection of artists and brands. The website has the feel of an online magazine thanks to features like an active social feed, a calendar of upcoming exhibitions, and a high-touch editorial page with biographies and artist statements. All transactions are performed using ether, the native cryptocurrency of the Ethereum network, in Newark, Delaware. Category: Digital art

Foundation, which debuted in February 2021, has hosted NFT sales of the popular internet joke. Nyan Cat, Pak's Final Record, and works by artists such Puffy Riot's Nadya Tolokonnikova, Aphex Twin, and Edward Snowden. The artwork of artists is arranged in a grid of cards, with hot auctions at the top of the page and highlighted artists following. Works are listed at a reserve price, and bids may be submitted for 24 hours, with a 15-minute extension if they are submitted in the last 15 minutes. Users must first set up a MetaMask wallet using Ethereum in order to create an artist profile, mint an NFT, or buy artwork from the website.

The location is Los Angeles.

- Category: Digital artwork

Mintable

owned by Marc Benioff and backed Time Ventures and billionaire investor Mark Cuban founded Mintable, a two-sided market place for buying and selling NFTs that is similar to eBay. Built on the Ethereum and Zilla blockchains, the website is integrated with MetaMask, where users may build up cryptocurrency walls. Creators have the choice to produce "gap-free" NFTs, short-run printed series, or conventional transaction-based products. After setting up profiles and loading their wallets, buyers may purchase advertised things or participate in auctions, with winners being notified through email.

"Location: Singapore"

Categories include digital art, photography, films, games, templates, and domain names.

The software development team of Dvin Finzer and Alex Atallah founded OpenSea in 2017, and it describes itself as "the first and largest market place for user-owned digital goods" on its website. OPENSEA now boasts more than 300,000 users, more than 34 million NFTs, and a trade volume of more than $4 billion as of October 2021. You may find anything on the market, which is filterable by price and sales status, from virtual real estate to sound loops from across the world. This weekend. A stat tab ranks sellers by volume, average selling price, and the number of items sold, just like a stock ticker. Buyers with wallets loaded with ether, USDC, DAI, or more than 150 other payment tokens may purchase fixed-price NFTs directly from sellers or place a bid on NFTs at auctions with an offer record recorded in the user's profile.

The location is New York.

- Categories include digital art, music, games, domain names, virtual worlds, sports, and collectibles.

NBA Top Shot is a licensed game that was released as a beta by DropperLabs in early 2020. It allows fans to collect and trade digital "moments" from the NBA. Moments are available in limited-edition sets with prices ranging from $9 to $230 or via open trade on a larger market. They include video highlights, player stats, and box emblems. Collectors may display curated collections, follow their favorite teams, and trade assets secured by the company's blockchain. NBA Top Shot has more over one million members as of May 2021, with 150,000 to 250,000 people logging in per day, according to CoinDesk.

Location: Vancouver, Canada.

Category: Collectible Sports Axie Infinity Developed by the Vietnamese startup Sky Mav, Axie Infinity is a Pokémoninspired video game where players gather zoo animals, engage in player-versus-player combat, and establish agricultural kingdoms. Between September 18 and October 18, 2021, Axie Infinity said that it has more than 23 million monthly players on average on its website. Characters and land parcels are encrypted as NFTs. They are available for purchase by gamers and collectors on an online market place, with some virtual land plots costing more than $20,000 and anamals selling for hundreds of dollars.

Vietnam's Ho Ch Minh City is the location of this video game.

SORARE SORARE is a cryptocurrency-based fantasy sports league where users may collect player cards as NFTs and use them in online competitions. The website contains 180 recognized clubs, including the Major League Soccer teams, and all transactions are carried out in Ethereum. Although fans may participate in the fantasy league by purchasing inexpensive digital players, excluding NFT collectibles outcompete others via using many players. For instance, a rare card of Kylian Mbappe, a forward for League One club Paris Saint-Germain, sold in December for $65,000. According to TechCrunch, Sorare raised $680 million in Series B fundraising under the direction of SoftBank's Vision Fund 2, valuing the firm at $4.3 billion.

The location is Para, and the category is sports collectibles.

VENLY With a user base of more than 200,000 gamers, VENLY's peer-to-peer NFT market place, now in beta, enables logged-in users to create, buy, and sell game characters, weapons, and collectibles without having to worry about first obtaining cryptocurrency. Users may connect their accounts to digital wallets to buy and sell assets from blockchain games like The Sandbox, Ethermon, and Vulcan Verse. Through a cooperation with Polygon, a platform for integrating Ethereum-compatible blockchain networks and cryptocurrency exchanges like Binance, the blockchain-based market place now accepts payments in U.S. dollars through PayPal.

Location: Antwerp, Belgium.

Category: Video games, metaverse

The Nfty Gateway

Nifty Gateway is a centralized U.S. dollar marketplace that collaborates with brands and artists to produce NFTs, a term that has been trademarked. Sales are organized around "drops," which are limited-time periods, often lasting three weeks, during which collections are made available. After a drop ends or an artwork sells out, funds may be refunded using the website's peer-to-peer marketplace. showcasing the work of artists and brands like as The site has a large volume and has a discovery page, a detailed statistics dashboard with sales and appreciation information, and a log of global activity. Beeple, BD White, Cam Hacks, Forbes, and Playboy are just a few examples of the high-profile brands it works with.

The location is New York.

Categorization: Digital Art

Zora Zora is a conventional auction house with an outwardly active mission: to assist artists in regaining the value that galleries, big brands, and bazaars have historically accepted as a standard for service and distribution. Customers may locate digital files for sale in the form of music, video, photos, GIFs, and text via connected Ethereum wallets like MetaMask, WalletConnect, and Coinbase. In addition to acting as a market place, Zora is an open-source protocol built on the ERC-721 standard, which is the most widely used for NFTs. Creators may purchase and sell NFTs everywhere that the protocol is integrated, and they can specify royalty rates for further sales.

The location is Los Angeles.

Category: Digital artwork

Decentraland, which self-brands as "the first-ever virtual world owned by users," brings the concept of the subway to its logical conclusion by letting users explore casinos, underwater kingdoms, and space portals while using a builder tool to develop land holdings and gather power and influence. The game, which can be played through a web browser or with a VR headset, serves as a self-contained marketplace where users can buy and sell land, cities, avatar apparel, and names registered on the Ethereum ledger. According to the NFT sales database NonFungible, the site had 196 sales totaling more than $491, 000 between October 11 and October 18, 2021.

Location: Bejing, China Subcategory: Video Games, Metaverse

Rarble Rarble is an NFT marketplace where users can browse, buy, and sell digital collectibles ranging from gummy bear GIFs to animated videos honoring sporting milestones like boxer Floyd

Mayweather Jr.'s unbeaten 50-0 record. The layout is similar to SPOTFY, with a scrollable stack of columns showcasing top sellers, popular collections, and live auctions. Rarible is now transitioning to become a decentralized autonomous organization and will soon be regulated by the Ethereum blockchain's rules, which provide open, permissionless usage. The most active buyers and sellers are given the opportunity to vote on platform updates and participate in management decisions via a governance token known as RARI.

The location is Wilmington, Delaware. Digital art, photography, music, games, the metaverse, and memories are categories.

The Sandbox With the stated goal of "disrupting the existing game makers like Minecraft and Roblox by giving creators true ownership of their creations as non-fungible tokens," according to a project white paper, The Sandbox is a video game where users may earn money by selling their experiences on the Ethereum blockchain. SAND cryptocurrency serves as the game's utility token and use charge. A web-based market place allows users to upload, publish, and sell items made using the 3D voxel modeling tool VoxEdt as NFTs. Purchased or produced creations may be placed on land parcels to change the game's mechanics via predefined behaviors.

The location is San Francisco. Category: video games and television

MakersPlace

MakersPlace is a gallery of digital artwork that is styled after creator collections and biographies. The home page includes brief films, lively motion graphics, and images of lunar landscapes, reimagined sculptures, and mythical gods. Each piece is issued, signed, and permanently recorded via the blockchain by the artist. The website is informative and simple to use because to its detailed artist profiles, freely accessible ownership records, and searchable tags. Work may be purchased via fixed price sales or digital auctions using a standard credit card. According to the website NFT-Stats, MakersPlace aged 119 NFTs between October 11 and October 18, 2021, with a trading volume of $901,700.

The location is San Francisco.

Category: Digital art, virtual reality, short film, motion analysis

Establishing Your Real Estate Goals

You have certain objectives in mind when you join the housing market. It doesn't matter whether your objectives are to retire early, run a massive real estate empire, or just have enough money to do so. You're into this with a clear goal in mind.

Remember that the real estate market moves quickly, and you must act quickly to take advantage of any opportunities that can slip by if you are not paying attention to what is happening.

You're going to need a strategy to implement your profit aim, whether it's to supplement your income so you can leave your work, save money for retirement, or simply have a little more money for whatever it is you want additional money for.

improving your income

In order to create the amount of money you want to in a year, you must first be able to define a goal objective. Make sure your objective is both realistic and reachable.

After that, calculate the average profit you may be able to make from each property over the course of a year. This is the time to do some research to discover how the local real estate market is doing.

This can let you track how sales in your region have developed and are developing, which will help you make sure your aim is reachable.

In order to determine the bare minimum of properties you must discover and manage each year in order to reach your objective, divide what you really want to earn in profit by the average profit per property.

Giving Your Job Up

You must first have the correct frame of mind if you want to totally invest in real estate and leave your career. Make a commitment to yourself to monitor your actions. Since the path to success will be difficult, it is important to make an effort to garner the support of your friends and family.

Real estate agent work requires a lot of time and effort. Having people that encourage you will aid in maintaining your motivation. Find out why you want to leave your job. Your choice will be motivated by emotion rather than logic.

This justification will provide you everyday motivation and drive to keep moving ahead.

Make future preparations. What will happen now that you have quit your job?

You'll need to create some kind of objective if you want to earn money and live each day. You will discover ways to increase the amount of money you generate from each transaction as time goes on and you continue to educate and develop your knowledge.

Make sure you have a strategy in place for whatever it is you want to do. You must have a strategy in place for how you will acquire rental properties if you want to have a large number of them.

Additionally, how would you manage all of your properties if you acquire more than you anticipated?

Will you hire any people or have a business partner?
You should take into account each of these factors while creating your business strategy. Unexpected situations that you cannot prepare for will always occur. The bulk of what you can plan for, however, you can prepare for.

100 percent passive income

A source of passive income is something in which you have no direct financial participation, such rental properties. Like non-passive income, passive income is subject to tax. The IRS, however, has a different perspective. Your portfolio's income would be considered passive income by some experts since it includes dividends and interest. These are all regarded as passive.

You must have several assets that still bring in income for you without tying up cash in order to make passive income from investing. In order to pay your mortgage and other property responsibilities, your cash flow should be enough.

Make retirement plans.

And everyone wants to have enough money in retirement to live comfortably. But how can we finance our retirement via real estate investing?
In the end, your monthly income will assist you in funding your retirement. You may put aside a portion of your income to contribute to retirement savings after paying the mortgage and

any other property-related expenditures.

When you purchase a structure containing several units, such as a duplex, and decide to reside in one side while renting out the other, you have purchased a multi-unit.

One advantage of having a multi-unit property is that you will have many revenue streams, so the loss of a tenant won't have an impact on you. However, if you have a triplex or quad, this will only function.

You'll be on-site in case anything goes wrong, which is one of the benefits. Once they get to know you personally, your renters will feel more at ease approaching you with maintenance requests for the property. In the event that you need to rent out one of the apartments that are currently occupied, this will help you retain the property's value.

Make a fortune with real estate:

You must first decide which route you will take.

Do you want to purchase and hold or repair and flip? Typically, at this point in their investing careers, individuals decide what they want to do and stay with it.

You may, however, do both since they will have different affects on the money you will make.

There are certain properties that are more suited for keeping than others for flipping.

But if you have both, you'll be able to travel more quickly. By making a tiny initial investment, you may practice investing; but, if you end up making more money than the other player, you will get more actively engaged in the game.

In general, your financial situation will improve if your investment portfolio has more units and diversity.
RISKS OF BOND INVESTMENTS ARE LISTED BELOW.

Credit risk
Remember the fundamental rule of securities: When loan fees are lower, security costs are higher, and when loan fees are higher, bond costs are lower. The risk associated with loan fees is that changes in financing costs (in the US or alternatively in other international business sectors) might reduce (or increase) the market value of the security you now own. The risk associated with loan fees, often known

as market risk, increases the more security you possess.

Let's look at the risks that rising loan costs bring with them.

Assume you paid $1,000 for a security with a 10-year maturity at a 4% yield rate today, with financing expenses rising to 6%.

If you wish to sell your 4% security before it develops, you will have to compete with newer securities that provide greater coupon rates. These securities with higher coupon rates reduce demand for more seasoned assets with lower revenue. A lower price for your share in the event that you decide to sell it would result from this decreased demand driving down the price of more established securities in the auxiliary market. It's possible that you'll have to sell your bond for less than you originally paid for it. Because of this, market risk is sometimes used to refer to loan cost risk.

New securities are also more tempting as a result of rising loan costs (since they earn a greater coupon rate). This results in what is known as "happenstance risk"—the risk that a better opportunity may present itself that you might not be able to take advantage of. The likelihood that a more lucrative investment opportunity may arise or that several other circumstances may arise that negatively impact your enterprise increases with the length of the bond's tenure. This is sometimes referred to as "holding-period risk"—the risk that a better opportunity may be overlooked, but that something may happen while you are holding a hold to adversely affect your supposition.

Administrators of security stores are under the same peril as individual bondholders. When financing expenses increase, especially when they do so quickly and sharply, the value of the asset's existing securities declines, which may hinder overall asset execution.

Call Danger

A security guarantor frequently calls security when financing costs drop, allowing the backer to sell new securities paying lower financing costs—therefore setting aside the guarantor cash. This is similar to when a property owner looks to renegotiate a home loan at a lower rate to set aside cash when advance rates decrease. As a result, security is routinely requested after reductions in lending fees. The security's manager receives an early reimbursement, but the financial supporter is rendered unable to find a comparable security with an equally alluring payout. An example of a call danger is this.

With a callable security, you most likely won't get the security's special coupon rate throughout the duration of the security, and it may be difficult to find comparable speculation paying rates that are higher than the first-rate. This is referred to as a reinvestment risk. Additionally, a callable security's premium installment rising after the call date has passed is debatable, and any increase in the security's market value could not exceed the call cost.

Time Risk
There is a number you should be aware of if you own securities or have money in a security shop. It is known as a word.

Even though it is represented in years, duration is not only a percentage of time. In light of everything, span indicates how much your security speculation's cost will likely change if loan costs increase or decrease. The more sensitive your security speculation will be to changes in borrowing costs, the greater the duration number.

Business analysts refer to the risk associated with the vulnerability of a security's cost to a one percent rise in borrowing costs as "length hazard."

Discounting Risk and Provisions for Sinking Funds

Bond guarantors are sometimes required to resign from a certain number of bonds under a sinking store arrangement, which is typically a component noted for bonds provided by contemporary and service companies.

This may be grown in a variety of ways, including by purchases in the secondary market or restricted purchases directly from bondholders at a predetermined price, also known as discounting risk.

Holders of securities susceptible to sinking assets should be aware that this increases the risk of reinvestment since they run the risk of having their bonds resigned before to development.

Risk of Default and Credit

It's likely that if you've ever given someone money, you considered the possibility of getting compensated. Some technological advancements are riskier than others. When you invest in bonds, the analogy holds true. You must prove that the guarantor's promise to pay back the amount and pay interest according to the agreed-upon dates and conditions will be upheld.

Although most U.S. Depository safeguards are thought to be free from default risk, most securities nevertheless run the risk of default. This suggests that the bond obligor will either be late paying lenders (including you, as a bondholder), pay a reduced amount that has been agreed upon, or, in the worst-case scenario, not be able to pay at all.

Using Rating Agencies to Evaluate Credit and Default Risk

Ten rating agencies have been designated as Nationally Recognized Statistical Rating Organizations (NRSROs) by the Securities and Exchange Commission (SEC).

These organizations gather information about the selected supporters, primarily financial information such as the guarantor's financial reports, and assign a bond's guarantor a letter grade ranging from AAA (or Aaa) to D (or no rating).

Each NRSRO uses its own assessment criteria and methods for the security rating that is awarded. The very cling is perfectly capable of obtaining a rating that contrasts, sometimes lavishly, beginning with one NRSRO then moving into the next. Although it is a good idea to compare a security's appraising across the many NRSROs, not all securities are assessed by each organization, and some securities are not even remotely appraised. In such circumstances, you can believe that it is difficult to evaluate the bond's guarantor's overall dependability.

Back off the dial when you see "High return"

Bonds are often divided into two broad categories: speculation grade and non-venture grade. The majority of the time, securities rated BBB, BBB, Baa, or above are thought to being speculative grade. Non-speculation grade securities are those that have an appraised value of BB, bb, Ba, or below. The terms "high return" or "garbage bonds" are also used to refer to non-speculation grade securities. Garbage securities often provide a higher return than investment-grade securities, but the higher yield comes with more risk, namely the risk that the bond's guarantor may fail.

Do not reach out.
Financial supporters who base their decision to buy a security on its yield are "going after yield," which is perhaps the most well-known error that financial backers make. The Grass Isn't Always

Greener—Chasing Return in a Challenging Investment Environment is described in FINRA's Investor Alert.

Risk of Expansion and Liquidity
Expansion hazard, also known as buying power hazard, is the risk that the return on securities won't increase with purchasing power. For instance, if you acquire a five-year security with an understandable 5% coupon rate but an 8% expansion rate, the purchasing power of your bond interest has decreased. All bonds, but particularly those that adjust to expansion, like TIPS, expose you to some expansion risk.

The risk of not being adequately prepared to find a buyer for a bond you truly want to sell is known as liquidity risk. The total level of trading activity is a sign of liquidity, or its lack. A bond that trades often on a particular trading day is much more liquid than one that trades just once each week.

a few of bonds, like U.S. Due to the large number of people interested in buying and selling these safeguards at any one moment, depository protections are relatively easy to market. These safeguards are flexible. Others swap far less often. Some bonds even wind up becoming "no offered" bonds, meaning they have zero chance of being purchased. These safeguards lack liquidity.

Financial backers may use FINRA's Market Data Center to monitor corporate securities trading activity and, in turn, liquidity. Financial backers may use the exchange information on the Municipal Securities Rulemaking Board's website to get knowledge about the liquidity of city securities.

Situational Risk

The majority of events that endanger company securities include mergers, acquisitions, used buyouts, and significant business restructurings; therefore, the term event hazard.

Changes in an organization's financial situation and potential may also be brought on by other events, which might lead to an adjustment in the bond's worth. These include a government investigation into potential wrongdoing, the untimely death of the CEO or other important directors of a company, or an item review. Energy prices, unidentified financial supporter interest, and global events are also occasion risk triggers. Occasion risk is very difficult to predict and might negatively impact bondholders.

Cheap Investments To Expand Your Portfolio

When you decide to start investing, it's crucial to remember that there are costs associated with doing so. We have so far discussed how much commissions brokers get from your investments. While it is reasonable in terms of the service they provide, the money for that comes from your earnings. The procedure is unfair as a result of this. All investment companies and stockbrokers rely on their clients for revenue. The worst aspect is that the majority of investors just consider it to be an inevitable part of conducting company. However, if you look closer, you'll discover that they earn far more than you realize.

Therefore, the focus of this chapter is on identifying the unintentional expenses of spending and how to account for them so that you don't pay a cent more than necessary. Frequently, this entails acting independently. For instance, some investors decide to engage in FOREX trading or day trading. In this approach, the costs they pay are less than what brokers charge.

Of course, we'll look at all sides of the debate so you can decide on investing in a way that's best for you. You need to make decisions that are beneficial for your family's welfare and your portfolio overall. In the end, this is the main motivation for your search for an investment.

The first thing to think about is if you want to pursue investing actively. Take this circumstance as an example to demonstrate the idea.

You are regarded as a leading expert in your subject. You may be a doctor, lawyer, engineer, or another profession. As a consequence, you get a good salary for your work. This implies that you will earn more money the more you labor. Every day you miss from work costs you money. You must decide how much a day or an hour of your time is worth in this circumstance. Would it make sense for you to take time off from your normal job to day trade if that were the case?

You can end up losing money.

Consider a top-tier lawyer who bills $400 per hour. It's likely that this lawyer would be better off employing a money manager to look after their finances unless they can earn $400 or more every day investing. They may arrange a weekly call with their fund manager if they truly want to be involved. They are able to monitor events in this manner.

Now think about the reverse. You have some free time right now. As a result, you've made the decision to start investing in order to increase your knowledge and your financial situation at the same time. Even if your hourly wage may not be $400, you still have an excellent work and a respectable income. You find day trading intriguing since you can fit it into your schedule. Additionally, trading may be automated so that you don't always need to be in front of the computer.

I'll give you a third example.

You consider day trading, FOREX, or even cryptocurrencies to be difficult topics about which you want to learn all you can. You don't really consider it a job and you don't do it out of a need for money. You consider it to be a teaching moment. As a result, you are drawn to the idea of managing your own assets and earning money. You are prepared to accept the challenge it brings as a result.

These instances all demonstrate different motivations for engaging in investment to varying degrees. Nevertheless, these are all illustrations of how you may still become an investor without sacrificing your way of life. You can succeed in investing whether you're a pricy lawyer or simply a regular person. All you need to know are the exclusive tips. Additionally, it's crucial to comprehend the principles of investing.

the expense related to investments

Understanding the costs associated with investment is a necessary component of learning the basics of investing. You will incur costs with your investments unless you are a venture capitalist that finances startup firms directly.

So let's examine each expense individually.

Fees for membership

You may need to pay a membership fee, depending on the fund you want to join. These costs, which are typically assessed yearly, help to keep the lights on. Brokers and financial institutions pay the majority of their overhead in this area. As a consequence, they must charge clients a fee for becoming members of the club. Your required payment will depend on the fund's kind. The most wealthy investors will probably spend a few thousand dollars a year to join the club. This charge, however, also guarantees that only those who are really eligible may join. It's really a means of promoting exclusivity.

You normally don't pay any membership fees when you join a fund via your neighborhood bank or investing company. Even if you did, the costs would not exceed a few dollars each year. That's nice to know, then. But you must account for that expense. You should thus ask your broker that question.

You will also have to pay an annual membership fee for the usage of your preferred trading platform if you decide to pursue day trading. Discount brokers sometimes don't impose any fees. They just generate that money somewhere else. You would still need to make a yearly payment of some type to keep the platform functioning, however.

Commissions

The majority of a broker's income comes from commissions. The majority of stockbrokers don't even earn the federal minimum wage; rather, commissions make up their entire compensation. Therefore, they won't be compensated if they don't sell. It's that easy. Stockbrokers are pushy because of this. They will constantly make every effort to upsell you. Furthermore, don't be shocked if you suddenly get calls from companies giving you fantastic incentives to switch to them.

What causes it to occur?

Brokers may leave one company for another, taking their customers with them. They get your name and phone number in this way.

Broker commissions typically vary from 3 to 6 percent. It resembles the usual fee for real estate agents. They are legally required to stay inside a particular range, which is the reason behind this. Otherwise, they would utterly gouge you.

Therefore, in addition to paying membership dues, you also have to pay your account manager commissions for managing your portfolio. Over time, these commissions might add up quickly. Discount brokers, however, should be avoided. They may be able to give you a rate of 3% or even less, but you need carefully do your research on these people since they can be operating their business out of a garage. Who knows what they're planning in that situation. Therefore, it is usually preferable to spend a little bit extra while making sure you are not taking on unnecessary danger.

Taxes

Oh, and the government must get its share as well. In this respect, you must be aware of both federal taxes as well as state taxes specific to your state. Investors often pay capital gains tax. This is the same plan used when selling a house.

The majority of brokers withhold taxes from your profits when you create a brokerage account. Not all of them, however, do. Therefore, this is something you should inquire about. You must report this income on your tax return and pay any taxes you owe if your broker does not withhold taxes from your profits. You may thus be liable for both income tax and capital gains tax. You may be eligible to deduct your capital gains tax from your income tax under certain schemes. Although this is helpful, you must apply for it. However, it's a choice you could make.

On average, you may anticipate paying taxes on short-term gains, or profits achieved over a period of more than a year, at a rate of between 15% and 20%. Depending on your income category, you may be hit with taxes on assets held for less than a year that range from 10% to 37%. In other words, taxes will eat up your gains if commissions and fees don't.

There is some good news, however. If your annual income is under $40,000, you could avoid paying capital gains taxes, particularly if your earnings don't go beyond your bracket. Therefore, if you earn a $50,000 profit, you'll be in trouble. In the range of $40,000 to $430,000, your bracket, you may anticipate paying roughly 15%. Over $430,000 will probably result in 20% taxation.

Some investors decide to hang onto their assets for as long as they can in order to avoid having to pay a large charge. This gives you the option to pay less or pay no taxes at all. For instance, depending on the plan you are under, mutual funds are not subject to taxes at maturity. If you remove money from a 401(k) before reaching retirement age, you won't be taxed at all. To think about are these two things.

Additionally, ask your broker whether they provide tax-exempt accounts. For extremely modest investments, there are retail accounts available. As a result, these accounts are free from taxes up to a specified amount. Investigating them makes perfect sense, therefore. You can benefit from accounts like IRAs and Roth IRAs, for example. Similar to 401(k)s in operation, they may provide far more flexible parameters, such as shorter investment periods or a cap on the amount of money you can remove each year without incurring any penalties.

How to Profit from Different Investments

Creating several money sources is one of the secrets to financial independence. A revenue stream is something that allows you to get money. Some generate a lot of money, whereas others don't. However, when you total them up, they really matter.

The idea behind developing several revenue streams is that the more sources of income you have, the simpler it will be for you to stop dependent on just one. When your only source of income—say, your job—is gone, your financial situation is completely destroyed. However, you have the chance to lessen your vulnerability to the ups and downs of the economy when you develop different income sources. Furthermore, losing one source of income, like your employment, won't cause your finances to collapse. It could hurt your finances, but it won't make it impossible for you to support yourself.

Building various income sources is a skill that successful investors excel at. Both passive and active behaviors are present. However, they are all helping to create a stable financial future. Let's investigate how you can make this work, then.

Let's start by assuming that you are employed. This will serve as your primary source of revenue for a time. This will be your primary source of income, from which you may develop your other sources of income. As a result, you must make sure that it continues to be stable for the foreseeable future. Making arrangements in case you need to locate a new work is a smart idea if you are uneasy about your future in your present position.

Decide which of the investment products offered here is ideal for you after that. For instance, you may not have much time to dedicate to direct investing if your calendar is full. Therefore, a more passive instrument might suit you well.

Additionally, check with your employer to see whether they match your contributions to retirement plans like IRAs and 401(k)s. We've explained why these investments won't make you wealthy, but they will help you earn money in the future. Therefore, it is the kind of investment you should make just in case.

Next, go over to your neighborhood bank or give your closest broker a call. Ask questions about the many investing alternatives they have available to you. A mutual fund or index fund can be a good option for you. Some of these accounts may be started with only $100 and regular deposits. These may sometimes be taken out of your paycheck on auto-pilot. So, it's definitely worthwhile to investigate.

You can research FOREX if you're up for getting your hands dirty. Either create a trading account with a broker, or start your own trading platform. Please be aware that it is strongly encouraged that you thoroughly research the market before venturing out into the realm of FOREX trading.

I would also want you to look into bonds. Bonds may be your best choice if you're searching for a secure, long-term investment. Many people who inherit money choose to purchase government bonds rather than corporate bonds. In order to guarantee that an inheritance may be handed down from one generation to the next, consider the following. Additionally, the largest bond risk is a government default. That is very improbable. The safest bond ranges from 15 to 30 years. Also, don't panic if you need to pay them in before the deadline. They are constantly marketable. Of course, depending on the market, you may lose money on them. Still, bonds might provide you a secure option if you are not in a rush to spend the money you have right now.

Regarding real estate now.

Real estate for businesses may be risky. In a booming market, occupancy rates are relatively high. Your investing intentions, though, may be derailed if the economy weakens. Single-family houses are the most difficult to rent out if you want to buy rental properties. Apartments are thus the greatest choices, particularly if they are reasonably priced.

Here is the error that people who want to invest in real estate make. They search for discounts. You see, a property is inexpensive for a purpose. It usually has to do with the state of the actual property. It could need a lot of effort, or it might just be flawed in some way. Other times, it's just situated in a terrible area. on terms of real estate, the saying "buy the best house in a bad block" is unwise. A solid rule of thumb is to always purchase "the worst house in a good block."

Ideally, you would have enough cash to pay for the house completely and have no debt associated with it. If you were to finance it, take into account your ability to make a down payment and the mortgage's monthly payment. Using such information, you can determine if the investment is worthwhile or not.

How so?

It depends on what the rent would cost on the open market. If you discover that the rent is much less than the mortgage payment, you wouldn't be generating much money from it. The ideal situation would be for the rent to pay the mortgage. So even if you lost money above the mortgage, at least you would have renters paying the mortgage.

Please keep in mind that purchasing real estate might be a risk, particularly if you aren't picky about the location. Therefore, bear this in mind while searching for real estate.

Making Money With ETFs
We have spoken extensively about exchange-traded funds (ETFs) throughout this book since they are popular across a wide range of sectors and asset classes. You may choose from a wide range of options as a result, making it simple for you to locate an investment that meets your requirements.

Investing in a stock ETF makes sense for you if you want to play it safe and not take on too much risk. These goods are available for a particular industry. You know a lot about the mining sector, for example. You may thus discuss the ETF's characteristics and the businesses it intends to invest in with your broker.

Additionally, if you are experienced with commodities like precious metals or crude oil, you may discuss your broker's investing strategy with them. In this manner, you might learn a lot about their strategies and how they intend to use your money.

It's also critical to comprehend the dividend rate, the commission, and any other unstated expenses. For instance, certain ETFs could need a minimum investment. If not, there can be a maintenance charge for the low balance. In other circumstances, you may need to make a minimum deposit to maintain your membership in the fund.

As you can see, there are a variety of requirements that you would need to satisfy in order to benefit from the fund. Additionally, it's crucial to research the fund's typical return rate before investing. You may then determine how much you can reasonably anticipate. Although no fund can promise you a particular return, having a range you can bank on is undoubtedly helpful.

We ask that you remember there are no promises. If you are shrewd enough to choose the appropriate asset class, there is a ton of upside to ETFs. Due to this, we will examine how to profit from ETFs in more detail.

How Etfs Make Money

Let's examine how the ETF itself generates revenue.

ETFs profit from an asset's rising price, regardless of the underlying asset the fund trades in. If the cost decreases, they suffer a loss. It truly is that easy. Therefore, brokers must take all reasonable measures to prevent being completely eliminated in the event of a significant drop in pricing.

In general, major changes don't occur until an unforeseen incident triggers a sharp decline in pricing. When this happens, brokers must take all reasonable steps to close out their position as soon as possible.

Let's use a well-known illustration to demonstrate the flexibility of ETFs.

You make the decision that you want to learn more about the oil industry. You then invest in an oil-based ETF. The fund manager or broker will make oil investments in this fund. This might be done by purchasing spot market direct purchase contracts or oil futures.
Let's now imagine that the price of oil increases as a result of higher demand throughout the summer. The broker then makes a tidy profit by selling all of the contracts they had been holding. All of a sudden, they make back their initial investment plus a healthy return. After then, the profit is distributed among the investors by the fund.

But here's the catch:

If you don't know how oil prices operate or how the market is doing, you'll believe your broker when they tell you that you earned a certain sum of money. If you are completely informed on market performance, you may call your broker and inquire about the fund's performance. From there, you can tell whether they're treating you unfairly. Even if you may not be able to get any knowledge about the fund's overall performance, you can at least determine whether a certain ETF is worthwhile to keep onto.

Let's imagine that a decline in demand and an increase in supply cause the price of oil to dive. This indicates that the broker's contracts are really worth less than they seem on paper. The broker is thus forced to get rid of them. If they are getting close to adulthood, this is very harmful. The broker's decision is therefore forced. They have to accept whatever price they can receive for their products. This implies that the fund suffers a loss. This causes you to lose money.

You may phone your broker and inquire about the problem if you are aware of the scenario. They will assure you that everything is OK, but at least your broker will be aware of your situational awareness. Depending on the kind of the fund at this stage, you may request a refund. You are forced to follow along if you are committed to that fund for a certain amount of time.

ETFs are profitable as a collective. Their returns are often higher than the stock market's average return. For this reason, starting with ETFs is a terrific approach to enter the world of investing.

Tips And Techniques For Etf Investing

Let's look at three foolproof methods you may use to increase the return on your ETF investments.

Recognize the ETF's nature. Investors are all too often persuaded to make an investment without fully comprehending the nature of the investment instrument. While this isn't always a negative thing, it does make it difficult to know what to anticipate. This is why you should inquire thoroughly before making a decision. The broker or sales representative you are conversing with is not worth working with if they are unable to respond to your inquiries. They ought to be willing to spend the time to allay your concerns if you already have a connection with them. Pay close attention to the contract's length, all payments, dividend distribution, and any taxes that may have been withheld. All of these should be taken into account before registering. Don't join up if any of these things doesn't persuade you.

Take a look at the foundational asset. Understand how the fund stands to gain money, regardless of whether the underlying asset is a cryptocurrency, stock, or any other kind of asset (for example, commodities). You are setting yourself up for a trip to the cleaners if you are unable to identify a means for the fund to generate revenue. This reinforces the conventional wisdom that you should only invest in companies you fully understand. So it is preferable to avoid a fund if its structure looks complicated. For instance, investors were sold mortgage-backed ETFs back in 2007–2008. These funds had the potential to generate income from the homeowner's debt. And have a look at the results. Therefore, it's crucial to complete your research before enrolling.

Fads should be avoided at all costs. Avoid a fund if you hear about one that everyone is investing in. Funds that don't publicize are the finest. Why? Good items, after all, sell themselves. Therefore, if you see that everyone is recommending investing in this or that, you should carefully consider if this investment is actually all that it's made up to be. Consider Bitcoin. Before the entire public joined the Bitcoin mania, early investors had already made a tidy profit. The guests who arrived last were saddled with the cheque at the conclusion of the celebration. You must always avoid receiving the cheque as the only recipient.

Overall, being suspicious of the majority of investments will save you a ton of trouble in the future. Potential danger will be obvious to you before it really affects you.

The Investment Armory

What sets successful investors apart from the rest? Your first assumption, "experience," is somewhat correct. We may, however, omit the element of experience since we think it is not necessary to have prior success in the stock market.

So what do we still have? You will need certain skills, knowledge, and even personality traits to succeed as a stock investor. As a consequence, the following are some of the things you'll need to earn money investing in stocks.

Essential Capabilities and Skills

Let's start with the qualities that are either inherent in you or those you will need to create for yourself. The three-piece suit and money will be your starting point as you begin to dress the part of an investor. Following that, you may start to build the following essential qualities of a stock investor:

Analysis

A stock market investor will do thorough study in order to remain competitive. This is crucial since trends and other outside economic variables have a significant impact on the stock market.

The ability to identify the approaches, plans, and tools required to react to a market trend provides a more practical justification for the significance of stock market analysis. Later on in this book, you will understand the essential traits of different market scenarios as well as how to react to them in order to survive. By using analysis, you may learn how to adjust your strategy as the market moves toward a certain condition.

The implication is that an experienced investor knows how to strike a balance between earning the correct amount of money and acting when it is required. While the second is done for survival, the first is done for profit. You can accomplish these two goals at once with the help of your analytical skills.

Research

Investments demand prudence, which is what sets them apart from gambling. You must do your research before placing a bet on anything.

Avoid the urge to acquire prospective stocks straight soon when you come across them in the market. You must first learn as much as you can about a company before investing in and trading stocks. This includes learning about its management and any trends that could have an impact on the company's success.

How comprehensive is research when it comes to investing in the stock market? You must keep up with any alterations in the economy, in the political climate, and in the statements made by other corporations if you want to be sure you are purchasing the right stock.

You must develop a love of reading charts and tables if you want to keep track of how stocks are doing. This is crucial during recessions because a knowledgeable investor may make money while others lose it. Having the right amount of information can, at the very least, help you make better decisions.

Calmness is a crucial but sometimes undervalued quality among stock investors. One mistake newcomers make when confronted with a challenge is to panic. As a consequence, during the economic crisis of the 2000s, you can still see pictures of distressed stock investors gnashing their teeth at the New York Stock Exchange.

Do not assume anything that you do not. There is no perfect escape from stress in high-stakes settings like the stock market. But when you're under a lot of stress, you're more inclined to do foolish things that make the situation worse.

In the past, anxious investors have too often sold all of their stocks at the first hint of a slump without realizing that the whole issue may have been resolved without their suffering losses. On the other hand, a cool investor adjusts their strategy to benefit from the unanticipated change in plans.

Records Administration

A stock investor must also keep a record of every transaction they make. This has two advantages. Having a record will help you maintain track of any investments you have made and their current performance, thus the first reason is for archiving.

The second one is private. If you keep track of your paperwork, you can at least monitor your development as an investor. How successfully are your strategies being put into practice? Which areas have you not yet investigated? Is it time to postpone your relationship? Your records will make that and other information available.

Discipline

I've spoken at length on the difference between investing and gambling since many people mistakenly think of the former as being the latter. The stock market is sometimes compared to a more affluent casino sans slot machines.

Making money shouldn't be your main objective as an investor in the stock market. This is so because buying, trading, and investing in stocks ensures that you will profit (or lose) money.

To live a long and healthy life should be your goal. You need to be in the market for as long as you can to really comprehend how it functions. Understanding how the market works can make it easier for you to profit from changes in the market.

This is crucial in circumstances when losses happen often. Almost all investors will endure a losing run due to events that are either out of their control or within their control. You can get through these difficult times with the majority of your assets intact and be prepared to resume generating money when the market returns with a little bit of self-control.

Tools and Resources

After dealing with the more private issues, it's time to think about the tools you may individually get to stay competitive in the market. Each stock market investor uses a different set of tools.

Here are some resources and technologies you should get acquainted with before you start investing to make things simple.

Capital

Investing should never be done without a sound financial plan, of course. Making money in the market is not always simple. Although there is a high danger of loss, there is no guarantee of profit. In conclusion, you can only profit from the stock market if you're ready to stake the same amount or more.

Being fully honest, it doesn't really matter how much money you have set up for stock investment. The notion is that you shouldn't ever start investing in stocks when your bank account is empty. But before you start investing, save at least $1,000 to be safe.

An exchange system

In essence, a trading platform is where you do all of your financial operations. Prior to going into the market, the site must be carefully considered. Here, you must assess the commissions provided as well as the admission requirements for the platform.

Some brokers employ trading systems with large commissions per trade, but they need a minimum account balance or a history of multiple profitable transactions before they would sign you up. In conclusion, they are ok, but not perfect for total newbies like you.

As an alternative, there are trading platforms out there that could work with your current setup. Even while the charge you must pay for your intermediary is relatively expensive, at $10.00 per transaction, TD Ameritrade, for instance, has no minimum account balance restrictions. With a $5 trader charge, Option House may be less costly, but it also provides more extensive trading choices and tools.

If your trading and investing skills improve, you may invest in more robust platforms like Interactive Brokers or the aforementioned Ameritrade platform.

Mobile applications

Genuine traders and investors must be mobile enough to bring their work with them. Thankfully, there are apps that let you manage all of your stock market transactions from a single smartphone.

These programs are widely accessible, which raises the following issue: How should you evaluate them?

You will need a wide variety of in-app tools and settings to get started. Pick a stock investing software that makes it simple to find, evaluate, and keep track of possible stock investments. Choose an app that enables easy switching between your desktop computer and mobile device through a single account system if you want to seem more intelligent.

Finally, choose an app with a reasonable subscription fee. For some investors, the

$20.00 price tag of certain mobile apps may be too much to bear. If you want to get an expensive app, be sure it has a number of functions that will make investing easier wherever you are.

Tools for Screening Stocks

If you are a novice, it could be difficult to find the stock that is a suitable match for your requirements. A stock screener may help you in this situation by helping you search the market for stocks that satisfy a set of criteria you create.

For instance, you may search for companies based on their share prices, market size, and expected dividend yield. Fortunately, screeners are a common function on most trading platforms and applications.

Compared to generic screening applications, certain specialised screening apps, like Finviz, provide more precise screening criteria. The basic services are free for all investors, but access to its additional features requires a monthly charge.

More charts, more charts, please

It's crucial to remember that it's difficult to put the stock market into words. It is preferable to approach this from a nonverbal standpoint since there is a lot of number crunching and computation going on here.

Charts are helpful in this situation because they lay out and connect numerous bits of data in a logical manner, making it easier to decide what measures to take. A quick look at a chart will show the direction of a company's performance, the current value of its stock prices, the trend it is following, and what could occur in that industry in the next hours.

There is a catch, however. If you are not acquainted with what to look for and what each term means, it might be challenging to interpret these charts. Keep in mind that these numbers change on a minute-by-minute basis as well, which suggests that stock charts have a rather limited useful lifetime.

Fortunately, there are several services available to help you understand the information with the fewest words necessary. To keep up with stock performance in real-time, you must subscribe to them.

Brokerages

Think of this as an introduction to the stock market. Because you are new to the industry, there is always a chance that you may grow confused and make mistakes. To reduce this risk, use a brokerage service to assist you locate the stocks you're searching for.

On the other hand, brokers charge a commission, which means that a piece of your gains will be used to pay other people in the end. By looking for a cheap brokerage that offers all the essential services at a lesser cost, you may save money.

The best brokerage alternatives right now for investors are Robinhood, TD Ameritrade, and Fidelity. It's a wise decision to choose a brokerage like E-Trade that may concentrate only on stock trading. In other words, it's important to remember that there are services out there that are both inexpensive and efficient. You have to spend more money on market research the less money you spend on high-quality services.

Investment Analysis

Along with its diversity, your investment portfolio's risks and opportunities must also be taken into account. An study of your portfolio can help you identify which assets, given the state of the market, offer the highest potential for dividend growth.

On the other side, portfolio assessments have the problem of being rather expensive. Unless you know where to look for free services, that is.

A website called Portfolio Visualizer offers a free examination of a user's portfolio using decades-old data models. They can help you perform simulations, locate interesting locations based on historical data, and use a range of mathematical tools to assess all of your present investments.

The strategy may terrify some individuals, but the outcomes are clear-cut. You may make greater use of your portfolio as a whole by utilising the data supplied, as opposed to only concentrating on certain items.

monetary ratios

The vast bulk of stock market information is numerical. Because of this, every investor's first task is to interpret any financial information that is provided to them. You may be able to find and isolate the information you need with the help of a financial ratio. They help you understand the statistics both as a whole and as separate data points.

There are many different types and sizes of financial ratios, but they always belong to one of the following classes.

What Good Is Investing In Bitcoin?

By 2021, investing in bitcoin might turn you into a multimillionaire. This implies that you could get nothing in the end. However, how are both real? Although investing in crypto assets might be risky, it can also be quite profitable.

You may buy bitcoin to have direct exposure to the demand for cryptocurrencies, but buying the stock of companies that have a lot of exposure to the market is a safer but somewhat less lucrative choice.

3.1 Is using cryptocurrencies secure?

Even while bitcoin is currently not entirely safe, other signs point to its long-term viability.

3.2 Cryptocurrency risks

Cryptocurrency exchanges are more prone to hacking and other illicit activity than stock markets are. These security flaws have resulted in severe losses for investors whose digital money was taken.

retaining bitcoin is more difficult than retaining equities or bonds, in addition. Despite the fact that Coinbase and other exchanges of a similar kind make it simpler to buy and sell digital assets like Bitcoin and Ethereum, many users still choose to keep their digital assets off exchanges due to the aforementioned risk of hacks and theft.

The usage of hardware wallets, paper wallets, and cold storage solutions like cold storage are not without their own set of problems for bitcoiners. You won't be able to access your bitcoin if you misplace your private key. The greatest risk is this.

A cryptocurrency project's success is not guaranteed by investment. Although there are a huge number of blockchain projects vying for the attention of the cryptocurrency community, scams are also very popular. There won't be many profitable bitcoin businesses.

Because of this, governments may start to see cryptocurrencies more negatively than they do as innovative technologies, leading authorities to take action against the whole industry.

Furthermore, investors are taking on extra risk because of the cutting-edge nature of cryptocurrencies. A large portion of the technology is still under development and has not yet undergone extensive testing in realistic scenarios.

The use of cryptocurrency

Cryptocurrencies and the blockchain industry are becoming more and more popular despite their inherent risks. The development of essential financial infrastructure has made institutional-grade custody services more widely available to investors. The management and protection of cryptocurrency assets is becoming more and more accessible to both experienced and novice investors.

By creating bitcoin futures markets, several firms are gaining direct access to the sector. Other companies, including Square, have together invested hundreds of millions of dollars in Bitcoin and other digital assets, in addition to financial powerhouses like Square and PayPal. Tesla bought $1.5 billion in Bitcoin at the start of 2021.

Despite the fact that a number of factors affect how risky cryptocurrencies are, the industry is advancing at a fast pace, as seen by the acceptance. Because of this, both small businesses and enormous organizations are attempting to enter the bitcoin industry.

Why should you purchase cryptocurrencies?

Several cryptocurrencies, including Bitcoin and Ethereum, are created with long-term objectives in mind. Any cryptocurrency project's long-term success isn't assured, but early backers might benefit significantly if it succeeds.

But for any cryptocurrency effort to be considered a long-term success, widespread approval must be attained.

3.4.1 Long-term investment in bitcoin

The network effect begins to act when Bitcoin overtakes all other cryptocurrencies, increasing demand for it. Many people refer to it as "digital gold," but it may also be used as a kind of virtual money.

The supply of Bitcoin is fixed, in contrast to fiat currencies like the US dollar or the Japanese yen. Investors believe that as a consequence, the value of cryptocurrencies will increase over time. There are 21 million Bitcoins in existence in all, but under central bank control, governments are free to print as much money as they choose. When the value of fiat currencies falls, it is anticipated that the value of bitcoin would increase.

Some believe that if Bitcoin is widely accepted as a form of electronic payment, it may one day become the first truly global currency.

3.4.2 Purchasing Ethereum with the long term in mind

Investors who wish to diversify their portfolios using the Ethereum platform may buy Ether, the native asset of the platform. Although Bitcoin remains the industry leader in terms of digital money, Ethereum is building a vast ecosystem of decentralized applications (or "dapps") on top of its global computing platform.

Due to the enormous number of dapps that have been released on the Ethereum platform, this platform may likewise experience the network effect and provide long-term, sustainable value. On the Ethereum platform, "smart contracts" may be used. These contracts automatically carry out the conditions written directly into their code.

On the Ethereum network, ether is collected from users for each smart contract that is performed. Smart contract technology, for instance, has the potential to totally disrupt new enterprises as well as industries like real estate and banking.

With increased use of the Ethereum platform, the value and utility of the Ether token rise. Investors who have Ether may directly profit from this if they think the Ethereum network will last a long time.

3.5 Is investing in cryptocurrencies a wise choice for you?

The financial world has been completely swept up by bitcoin trading since its inception in 2009. The use of digital currency is expanding all around the world. The Chainalysis 2021 Global Crypto Adoption Index ranked India second in terms of the adoption of cryptocurrencies globally.

Due to the historical lack of correlation between Bitcoin and the stock market, investing in cryptocurrencies is a fantastic method to diversify your portfolio. As cryptocurrencies like bitcoin and others gain popularity, they can make a strong complement to a well-rounded financial portfolio. Every cryptocurrency you invest in should have a solid investment thesis explaining why it will endure.

If buying cryptocurrencies seems too risky, there are other ways to profit from their increasing value. You may buy stock in well-known cryptocurrency companies like Coinbase and PayPal or invest in futures on a market like CME Group. Even while investing in these companies might be profitable, it doesn't provide the same upside potential as doing so directly in cryptocurrencies.

But if you're interested in cryptocurrencies (or "crypto") but unsure of where to start, the details below may be able to assist you in determining whether or not cryptocurrency is the correct choice for you.

being in control of your resources

The decentralization of cryptocurrency trading enables you to own and maintain your assets without requiring outside interference. Dealers are thus free to earn as much as possible by using the prevailing exchange rates.

assets that don't cause inflation.

Digital money, such as bitcoins and other cryptocurrencies, is very scarce. They are thus seen as deflationary assets, and as a consequence, their purchasing power increases with time. Any cryptocurrency's total supply is limited by an algorithm.

Safety and openness:

Cryptocurrencies have gained a lot of popularity because to its open-source and publicly verifiable technology. Indian cryptocurrency exchange ZebPay, founded in 2014, has a lengthy history. On it, you may exchange bitcoins in a secure and safe manner.

a top-notch long-term investment choice

Long-term investments in cryptocurrencies are seen to be especially profitable despite the market's turbulence and volatility. They could be helpful as a means of post-retirement savings or as a safety net in the case of a serious economic catastrophe.

Flexible and independent trading

Since crypto trading is accessible around-the-clock, traders may trade whenever they want. Other cryptocurrencies like Ethereum,

Dogecoin, and Ripple further increase the possibility for wealth building and portfolio diversification.

outstanding possibility for growth

The most discussed subject of the year was investing in Bitcoin and other cryptocurrencies. The New York Times, Wall Street Journal, and CNBC were awash with reports of people becoming millionaires extremely quickly.

But after January 2018, the cost of Bitcoin fell by 63 percent. The bull market in Bitcoin had come to an end, and the bubble had burst, according to the media, which reinforced this opinion.

Given that many billionaires had invested in bitcoin at the time, this tune was especially intriguing. Despite having previously referred to bitcoin as a hoax and threatened to fire any J.P. Morgan workers seen trading in it, Dimon has now emerged as one of the fund's most active investors. Following Dimon's remarks, Bitcoin's price fell by as much as 24%, and sure enough, J.P. Morgan and Morgan Stanley started buying for their clients at steep discounts.

This story isn't the only one in the crypto industry. For instance, barely eight weeks after denouncing Bitcoin at the World Economic Forum and labeling it a "bubble" in January 2018, billionaire hedge fund manager George Soros authorized his $26 billion family office to start buying cryptocurrencies.

Soros attributes a significant chunk of his success to "reflexivity". In other words, this theory contends that investors only base their decisions on what they believe to be the truth. Soros once said, "The degree of distortion may vary." It's hardly apparent in certain circumstances, but rather evident in others... Every bubble has two elements: an underlying trend that is true in the real world and a false impression of that trend.

The majority of people are unaware of what is occurring in the bitcoin sector. And the majority of individuals are uncertain about the future direction of the price. Prices are considerably more likely to drop when the major players do it for their own financial gain since the majority of market observers tend to follow market noise.

Investing In Options: A Guide

Options are often regarded as the safest investment instrument. You will learn the fundamentals of options investing in this chapter, along with the techniques used by professionals.

What are your choices?

It is a contract that grants the right to sell or buy an asset at a certain price to the holder. It is crucial to remember that this is a right rather than a duty. Options are a kind of asset like stocks. They also have traits and words that are well defined.

Options to put and call

There are now two categories of options:

Put options provide the holder the opportunity to sell a certain amount of an asset (a contract often comprises 100 shares of an asset). The sale price, commonly known as the strike price, has already been decided. Additionally, the transaction must be completed quickly since options have expiry dates.

Call options provide the holder the right to buy a certain amount of an asset at a specific price in a preset volume. Call options also have expiry dates, meaning the purchase must be completed before then. The option contract contains this information.

The Advantages of Alternatives

Options provide three key advantages. Which are:

Options may be used as a kind of protection for your financial portfolio. For instance, if market prices are very volatile, you may buy protection put options. These options may protect you against unexpected price declines, which will protect your long-term investments and earnings.

Utilizing leverage enables investors to purchase assets for less money. Speculative or short-term investors often make use of this advantage.

Quick Gains - Risk-taking investors may utilize options to profit on price swings. The investor need just wager on whether the market price will remain inside a certain range or not while using this approach. This is a kind of "volatility trading."

8 Successful Option Investing Techniques

The Married Put is a method where an investor who owns or acquires a certain asset also invests in put options to safeguard his investment. The amount of the assets he wishes to safeguard must equal the value of the options. Investors often choose this tactic when they are certain that prices will increase. Married put options shield the assets against unexpected and/or brief price drops.

The bear put spread involves the investor purchasing put options at a certain price and then selling the same quantity of puts at a much lower price. The expiry date for these choices must be the same. They also need to be used on the same object. This tactic is often used when the market is "bearish" (i.e., when prices are low and market participants are pessimistic about future performance). This technique is well-liked by investors since it offers a decent chance of profit and some loss mitigation.

The Bull Call Spread requires the investor to buy call options at a predetermined cost. Then, at a considerably greater price, he sells the same quantity of call options. These call options have similar expiry dates and must be used on the same asset. Use this strategy if you believe that the price of your selected asset will rise during a bull market (when prices are high and investors are upbeat about the market's performance).

The Protective Collar may be used by simultaneously buying put options that are out of the money and writing out-of-the-money call options. The same asset must be covered by each of these choices. A put option with a strike price below the asset's market value or a call option with a strike price above the asset's market value are both considered out-of-the-money options. Once they have made large gains, investors adopt this method. Without having to liquidate their assets, this plan enables individuals to safeguard their earnings.

The Long Straddle is a trading method where investors simultaneously buy a put and a call option. The same asset must be used to implement these options. They must also have the same strike price and expiry date. If you are positive that the price of an asset will change but unsure of whether it will go up or down, you must adopt this investing technique. You will experience little losses and almost limitless potential rewards with this method. Your potential loss is only capped at the entire cost of the options you purchased.

The Long Strangle is when a trader purchases both a put and a call option on the same security. These options have the same expiry dates but have different strike prices. The striking price of the put option must be less than the price of the call option. Additionally, nothing of these choices can be profitable. If you believe that the price of your selected asset will fluctuate sharply, you must use this method. The losses will be much less than those associated with the Long Straddle approach since the options involved here are out-of-the-money.

The Bear Put Spread and the Bull Call Spread are combined into one strategy known as the Butterfly Spread. In addition, three distinct pricing must be established. For instance, a trader may buy a call option at the lowest strike price, sell it for more money, and then sell another call option for a lot more money.

Investors see the Iron Condor as one of the most intriguing possible techniques. In this case, the investor must hold both a short and a long position simultaneously. Two strangling strategies are used to do this. That implies that you will need to use the Long Strangle tactic twice. While the second use should concentrate on carrying out your long-term ambitions, the first usage should be centered on generating immediate income (short-term).

How To Invest For Cash Flow

1. the many investment types
2.
3. I want you to immediately start making a profit on your first investments. I am aware that you are just starting out, that you probably don't have much money to invest, and that the benefits of investing are still purely hypothetical at this point. I believe you will have even more incentive to invest if I can help you generate interest that you may realize as cash in hand in as little as a year. For me personally, this was the tipping moment when I began to understand that investing meant more than simply setting money aside for the future. It implied that I would start to see results in a matter

of weeks, months, or even years. You won't have to wait much longer than I did to reap the rewards of my work.

4.
5. This chapter contains investments that provide the quickest rate of interest accrual, allowing you to see your money increase in real time. These investments also offer very distinct pay out points where you might realize your money in hand at a distinct time that you will choose. These investments are divided into traditional and non-traditional investments. Conventional investments will demand a larger initial investment, take longer to pay off, but will provide significant interest. However, you will start to see interest in your hands in as short as thirty days. Unconventional investments will take more

hands-on effort to manage. I would invest in both sorts of investments for the greatest outcomes, but if you have a limited amount to start with, attempt the unorthodox ones to earn more interest before moving on to more lucrative conventional endeavors.

6.
7. A Word About Saving
8.
9. You saw in chapter one how someone may rapidly increase the amount of their nest account by earning only 4% interest annually. Savings were necessary for this to succeed, however. Keep in mind that the interest that will accrue depends on the size of your initial investment. Since you're just getting started, you can't only depend on interest to expand your account; you'll need to make a sizable investment in order to

increase interest as quickly as possible. I advise you to save part of your money in fairly conventional methods, such as by simply setting away some money each and every week from your income, to hasten the rate at which you are earning interest. Make significant investments that will earn interest with this money every few months or at the end of each year. Once you have a sizeable account, you will discover that the interest you are earning is far more than simply saving a few dollars every week, but in order to get there, you will need to focus on saving in advance.
10.
11.   Standard Investments
12.
13.   stock dividends
14.

15. General Motors is great. I have never had a GM vehicle, and I don't really adore their automobiles, but I am completely intrigued with the brand. They paid over 4% in dividend interest last year. Working with stock market corporations that offer dividend interest is one of the primary investing methods. The sole prerequisite for receiving this interest is that you must be a stakeholder in the firm. It is interest that is paid to investors. You will be compensated with a dividend interest for each share of GM stock you own. In this instance, the interest earned is extremely substantial at over 4%. Understanding that your base investment is a two to three year investment and that the amount of money you may generate from your investment is directly related to how many

shares of a firm you hold is the key to dealing with dividend interest. Don't be too concerned about the lengthy requirement; you will still be receiving dividend interest at least once every year. I must note two very crucial characteristics of dividend interest: first, while being a stock market investment, it is not a very dangerous one. Two, although you have access to a whole other kind of investment—the shares themselves—by holding shares of a corporation, you are also receiving income on those shares.

16.
17. Although the idea behind dividends is straightforward, many Americans often struggle to describe precisely what they are and how they work. They want to make sure that you keep your stock shares when

you invest in a firm on the stock market. The corporation may have the option to split its stock, create shares, and raise the overall worth of the company when the market becomes competitive for purchasing additional shares of the company. This is true because a company's market capitalization, which is determined by the stock price multiplied by the total number of shares sold, equals the whole worth of the business in a technical sense. The company's main goal is to keep investors satisfied. There are two fundamental approaches to taking this action, and they complement each other well for investors. The first is that they just raise the company's worth, which increases demand for its stock and raises the price of it. A firm like Apple is really successful at this

because, even though their actual dividends were fairly modest only a few years ago, they were able to keep investors on board because of how rapidly the stock was rising. Knowing that the stock will likely increase in value, an investor would buy it with the intention of selling it later. Google did not have to distribute dividends regularly either in the early to mid-2000s. Their business was expanding at such a rapid pace that investors were drawn in just by the rising stock value. The luxury of having a stock expand fast, or at least swiftly enough to draw a growing number of investors, is not something that most firms can afford.
18.
19. Large, well-established businesses like Apple and Google must adopt a different

strategy to retain investors since these businesses have consistent profitability but haven't done anything to revolutionize markets or technology. They encourage shareholders to keep onto their equity by paying dividends. Given that dividends pay out a certain amount of money per share, the size of an investor's dividends increases with the number of shares they own in a corporation. This encourages investors to buy as much stock as they can in order to get higher dividend payments right away. This is one of the main investments that trusts employ to illustrate how much these dividends pay. Trusts like to utilize very low-risk assets with a reasonable degree of assurance that they will be able to generate interest. Trusts might have confidence in the security of their assets by dealing with dividend companies, or rather stocks that are widely recognized for paying dividends to share holders.

20.
21. The two strategies used by firms to persuade investors to keep onto their shares are not mutually exclusive, and both may be profitable for us as investors. Depending on how the firm pays out dividends, if you buy in a dividend stock like GM or American Airlines Group, you may start receiving money every three to twelve months. You also have a windfall of prospective revenue from the sale of the shares at your disposal. In general, you may anticipate that over a sufficient amount of time, a company's stock will increase. As a result, you get interest payments each year in

the form of dividends. However, after a period of time, you may also decide to sell your original investment, generating a sizable return on your capital all at once.

22.
23. New investors may find it unsettling to consider investing in the stock market, but in reality, we are making safe, long-term investments. For people who have not made many personal investments, there is a prevalent perception that the stock market is the wild west of investing, where fortunes can be made and lost in a matter of days. The stock market is really far more stable than most people realize, and over time, you may anticipate the market as a whole to appreciate in value. Due to the severe recession and financial crisis of 2008 and 2009, the Dow Jones has more than

quadrupled in value in only the previous fifteen years. Working with reputable, reliable firms is the key to making safe stock market investments. For further confidence, choose companies that pay dividends so you can start earning right immediately. The best way to generate stable income from investments in the stock market is to invest and then sit back; investments that require constant stock monitoring, such as those made by day traders, are riskier and are likely where you first developed your perception of the stock market as being extremely dangerous.

24.
25. The only major drawbacks to this investment are two. One is that you need to own a sizable number of shares of a firm in order to make a lot of

money right away. More precisely, I would anticipate that you would make, give or take, $300 per three months on a $5,000 market investment. Even if you are only able to purchase a small number of shares, keep in mind that you may sell them at a later date to generate additional revenue beyond the dividend payments' immediate cash value. The second issue is that there are sometimes financial crises of various degrees, even if the market will increase in the long term. Both the dividend payments you get and your capacity to obtain interest on stock sales would be affected by this. The best course of action in this situation is to stay in the market and wait it out. Although there is a little chance that this may happen, it is a danger to be aware of.

26.
27. Actual Estate
28.
29. After the 2008 housing crisis, there was some discussion over whether renting an apartment or house could be a better option than buying one. This isn't accurate today. It makes significantly more sense to own your home than to merely rent it in the majority of American cities and towns. Of course, there are rare situations when this isn't true, such when someone wants to relocate, but for the great majority of Americans, house ownership just makes sense. Even if you don't live there, the interest you can earn on a house is among the highest of any investment you can make. In addition to providing a place to live, a house is useful because of the significant profit it may

provide when it is sold. This is a long-term investment, but in certain regions of the nation, buying real estate may practically double your money in only five years. For instance, you may discover that homes are really appreciating at rates of up to ten to twenty percent per year by looking at the most populated places, where new inhabitants are coming in at the quickest rates. These cities include Austin, Texas, and San Francisco, where you may earn a ton of money within a few years. The crucial factor is that these cities are now becoming excessively costly, making it difficult to purchase a property in the current environment. For the majority of Americans, it would be preferable to just own a property in their neighborhood, depending on whether they use it or not, and sell this after five to ten years.

There is still hope if you want to invest in a city that has had rapid expansion in recent years but where home prices are still relatively low if you want to earn a lot of money very fast. I look to areas like Saint Louis and Minneapolis, where the housing market is ripe and the population is increasing quickly.

30.
31. A property does not have to be a long-term investment for interest to start collecting on it. Renting a home that you have purchased is a simple and straightforward approach to start earning money from your investment. This goes deeper than just purchasing a home and selling it afterwards. By doing this, you not only contribute actively to the financial success of your house but also create a new source of revenue for it. You can

effectively sell a house you've bought for a lot of money if you rent it out, and you can also collect rent from tenants in your properties. Although it won't be a viable choice for everyone, many investors may find success with it since it is a significant investment that begins to pay off right away.

Furthermore, there is worth in things other than merely a home or an apartment. The value of the land itself is often fairly high and will continue to rise. The wonderful thing about this is that the investment costs are far lower than those for a house, and you have no commitment to construct anything on any property you buy, so you may keep the deed and sell it at a later time. In certain areas of Florida, I am aware of a few investors who got engaged in this. They would purchase vacant lots and keep onto them for a while, paying land taxes and generally losing money, until they had the opportunity to sell the property to either someone. These sales would come from either private people looking to construct a house on it or, much more profitably, a business looking to create a housing development. This is a riskier investment since it is not always certain that your land will increase in value. However, the entrance barrier is much lower, and it's not like you can't predict with any degree of accuracy what land in your region will be valuable in the future. When someone approaches you wanting to acquire that property, looking into vacant lots—which many people consider undesirable—and making a purchase is a terrific strategy to guarantee future revenue. The only uncertainty is how long it will be until the land appreciates in value.

TRUST FOR INVESTING IN RESIDENCES

It is quite costly to invest in real estate on your own, but there is a method to reduce this expense by using a real estate investment trust. These are associations of individuals who combine their resources to purchase real estate. Typically, members either vote on a property or a central manager makes the acquisition. Similar to how an individual might benefit from a property, these organizations earn money. The gains are divided among all the investors if a property is purchased and then sold.

This is a fantastic method to earn money from real estate investments without having to participate in a project as the only investor. Additionally, it provides access to certain interesting alternatives that you would not otherwise have. One benefit is that you have access to a set of abilities that your other trust members also possess. While choosing a property that will appreciate in value might be a difficult endeavor for an individual, working on this process as a group can provide better outcomes. You can make better decisions because you have access to a far wider variety of information than you do alone. Second, the size of the property and, thus, the interest, may grow significantly. You may purchase homes in areas of your community where demand is presently high and where you anticipate a rise in demand in the very near future. This enables you to devote less time while still earning a lot of interest. The ability of the group as a whole to fund property renovation is the third, and perhaps most significant, characteristic real estate trusts provide. This crucial function of real estate investment trusts is far more difficult for an individual to do out. A group will purchase a home that requires repairs and upkeep in order to be marketable. Then, they will either repair the property themselves or engage a team to do it. A real estate trust might often include twenty or more members, many of whom have repair expertise. They only become a member of the trust to obtain access to a larger capital reserve. Although it is not unusual for these trust members to have a somewhat bigger share of the earnings since they worked harder, the profit from a property that has been improved should not be underestimated. While it is on a lesser scale with a real estate trust, there are whole companies that run on this concept, and it is still a fantastic chance to make income on your investment.

Finally, if a real estate company decides to rent out homes, they are quite adept at collecting rent from renters. Maintaining a few properties that are leased to renters becomes lot simpler when ten to twenty individuals collaborate. It resembles managing a company in several ways, but on a much smaller scale. Because these trusts eventually would need to recruit outside staff, which would reduce the trust's income, these organizations typically only have one or two tenants at most. This is a fantastic opportunity to get a return on your investment right now and get assistance through the challenges of renting out houses. You also have access to everyone's knowledge and expertise inside the real estate trust, just as with other elements of the trust, which makes the whole endeavor much simpler.

About a year ago, I started participating in a local real estate trust, and it has turned out to be one of my best financial decisions to date. The real estate trust achieved something that is extremely hard to do with other investments by returning 150% of my original investment in a year. You cannot expect most real estate trusts to achieve this level of success, and our market was at a distinct advantage because of an upsurge in local business. Our trust has enough funds to purchase and sell houses pretty rapidly, as well as to rent two properties, and there are many people and families seeking for homes. Our current goal is to purchase a house, make just minor repairs to it, and then sell it after a short period of time. For instance, we spent $250,000 for a house last spring. To renovate one of the bathrooms, repair the kitchen's tiling, and install French doors to the rear of the property, we invested an additional

10,000. Since no one in my trust is particularly handy or capable of doing this sort of job readily, we definitely overpaid for the work. As a result, we had to engage outside contractors, who are now quite busy due to the high volume of requests in our region. About nine months after we bought it, this house ended up selling for $370,000. As far as I'm aware, this is the most profitable investment our trust has ever made. However, it only goes to show what can happen when a property is bought and some effort is put in. It's difficult to find an investment that will return this much back. We earned around $90k overall after taxes, which left me with a profit of $5,200.

Your ability to participate in a real estate trust in your community will be greatly influenced by your social networks, the size of your town or city, and the amount of money you have to invest. As a community investment fund that later specialized in housing and development, our trust had its beginnings. You need at least $10,000 to join our trust, which is a significant financial commitment for many. However, the advantages of a trust much outweigh the disadvantages, therefore I would advise anybody looking to invest in real estate to use this strategy. If you have the capacity, I would even advise creating your own trust since the money is so valuable. Using the rising property prices in your neighborhood as evidence will make it simple for you to persuade others of the benefits of pooling your funds to buy real estate. This sort of enterprise also requires a very little amount of time overall, making it an excellent investment that will use up very little of your time.

www.ingramcontent.com/pod-product-compliance
Lightning Source LLC
Chambersburg PA
CBHW050244120526
44590CB00016B/2211